洞月亮

CAVE MOON PRESS
YAKIMA 中 WASHINGTON

2018

In Praise of Central Heating

"Central Heating" is a profoundly generous collection of poems: moving, insightful, as it embraces both empathy and peace.
—**James Bertolino**, author of
Ravenous Bliss: New & Selected Love Poems

Washington state poet Betty Scott has mastered many poetic formats and styles of poetry for her book, "Central Heating." Savour it slowly for its wisdom, then reread to dance to its beat. In her short poems, her quick reversals engage us, "love that unites us, also unties us." In contrast, she uses a chorus, ironic questions and philosophical pleas to protect Mother Earth, "turn around for Earth runs this race track/ her foot-falls on our back" in "Simply, Simplify." Sometimes emotional contrasts toss one over a waterfall to find clarity in the balancing of life: "like joy and sorrows, you left without goodbye." Her similes are fun for writers: "syllables bite like alligator teeth." Betty Scott has created a fine book with many appeals from intimate family life dramas to universal questions of "Why me? What next?" often tempered by her ironic tone.
—**Bernice Lever**, author of *Small Acts*, Black Moss Press, 2016, and BC, Canadian Peace Poet

Betty Scott travels *beneath sadness and joy* ("A Courtroom and a Waterfall") to know the language of the poem and in that place every voice matters: daughter, wife, doe and faun, dogs, dry creek beds, fathers, sisters, worms, and the earth itself.
—**Darrell Bourque**, former Louisiana Poet Laureate, author of *In Ordinary Light: New and Selected Poems; Megan's Guitar and Other Poems from Arcadia;* and *Where I Waited*.

I am so honored to commend to you "Central Heating" Betty Scott's inspired collection of poetry. Scott's poems remind me of the epic moments I might miss in what might so easily seem the minutiae of the day, and the tender details that humanize and consecrate the larger-than-life occurrences. Most of all her poems never fail to captivate, to move and connect me with something essential and sacred.
—**Reverend Doug Wadkins**, Unitarian Universalist minister

Betty Scott's poems explore worlds: the natural world; the world of family and community; the spiritual world; most importantly—that mysterious world of the self. Their reach is wide, yet they speak with a distinctly personal voice. That voice is humane, grounded in wisdom. It is the voice of a writer who has lived fully, who understands pain and joy, passion and compassion. In her foreword, Scott asks: *Does poetry matter?* Her poems are a moving response to that question. They are brave poems. They celebrate life.
—**Ed Stover**, Yakima Coffeehouse Poets

In "Central Heating" Betty Scott embodies Henry James's admonishment that the writer should be someone "on whom nothing is lost!" Nothing is too small or insignificant—a stalwart pansy poking through cement, a windshield-hugging lady bug ("So regal in her coat of black and red")—or too large (war, racism, ecological devastation, "our cruelties [that] breed disdain / for precious living things") to escape her compassionate, questioning, ardent attention. As the title poem reminds us, the "sol[ution] for earth and self" lies within us.
—**Lisa Russ Spaar,** author of *Orexia: Poems*

Betty Scott's poems come bravely to the heat of a central question: "how does the spirit / stay alive?" They show that the spirit's livelihood may depend on vivid consideration of the surprises gleaming in the places where "the infinite and minuscule breed," even among the deaths and demolitions that closely live with us. These are the "poems as prisms" of one who knows that love is a splintered thing, and yet to "listen kindly" can lead us to the "earthworms / plucked from grief's soil." Is it an accident that "soil" almost rhymes with "soul?" In this book, in which the upkeep of attention feels like a matter of public health and Scott's cultivation of a garden of forms brings intent and inventive music to poems of history and ecology, I don't think so.
—**Zach Savich,** author of six books of poetry, teaches at the University of the Arts in Philadelphia.

Central Heating

Poems that Celebrate Love, Loss and Planet Earth

Betty Scott

月亮
CAVE MOON PRESS
YAKIMA 中 WASHINGTON

Acknowledgements

The author wishes to acknowledge gratefully the periodicals or recordings in which several of these poems first appeared: *Bellowing Ark*: "Dry Creek Beds and Streams," "Savings"; *Borders*: "After His Sister Died"; *Chuckanut Writers Conference*: "The Playground"; *Cirque Journal*: "A Northwest Winter's Dream"; *Clover*: "Tree Reflections"; *Floating Bridge Press Pontoon*: "Thirty-six Lines in Defense of Clutter"; KMRE: "As I Woke from a Dream," "My Dog Barks," "What Sarah Couldn't Say to Abraham"; *Kumquat Challenge*: "Between Capricorn and Cancer," "Roots and Seeds"; *Labyrinth*: "A Courtroom and a Waterfall," "Ode to Butter"; *Noisy Water*: "An Earth Year Blessing"; *Peace Poems II*: "May Peace Become Us"; *Sue Boynton Poetry Contest*: "My Dog Barks"; *Soundings Review*: "Flirting at the Neighborhood Bakery"; *World Peace Poets*: "A Poet Prays for Peace"; *University of British Columbia Library*: "A Poet Prays for Peace"; *Yishar Koach: Forward with Strength, The Story of Shoah Survivor Ferdinand Fragner*: "Dear Fred," "After Words I," "After Words II".

The Magic Garden oil on canvas, 2017, 48 x 58, is the cover art by Alfredo Arreguín.
Various Mandalas pen and ink by Doug Johnson

© Copyright 2017 Betty Scott
All rights reserved.
Artwork by: AlfredoArreguín and Doug Johnson
Book Design by Doug Johnson

ISBN: 978-0692135600

Central Heating

Poems that Celebrate Love, Loss and Planet Earth

A Note of Thanks

It takes a village to affirm the industry of poets, poetry and the arts. Bellingham is that village, a thriving community of creative expression. Thanks to the generosity, spirit, and talents of Doug Johnson, Alfredo Arreguín and JP Falcon Grady. Thanks to my children, parents, siblings, cousins, aunts and uncles; they are the soil out of which my poems grow. Thanks to reader-editors Linda Conroy, Andrew Shattuck McBride, Kathleen McKeever, and Rob Stoops.

Thanks to Zach Savich, a fine, fine Iowa Summer Writing Festival instructor. Thanks to Jim Bertolino and Anita Boyle, often at the center of poetry and art in Whatcom County. Thanks to Laura Kalpakian, Cami Ostman, and Red Wheelbarrow Writers. Thanks to Carla Shafer and friends at Chuckanut Sandstone Writers Theater. Thanks to committee members who run the Sue Boynton Poetry Contest since 2006. Thanks to SpeakEasy Poetry Series, Luther Allen and Judy Kleinberg. Thanks to Ron Leatherbarrow and the Poetry Club and David M. Laws and the Word Nerds Writer's Group. Thanks to Wilfred Woods (1919-2017), Rufus Woods and The Wenatchee World, a family-owned newspaper, my training ground. Thanks to Poet Laureates Tod Marshall and Elizabeth Austen for their inspiring travels, their artistry at work honoring resilient spirits.

Many people and institutions resonate with the discipline and practice of creative and inclusive communities. Thanks to Western Washington University's graduate writing program. Thanks to Rev. Doug Wadkins, Rev. Paul Beckel, Beth Brownfield, Rev. Barbara Davenport, the readers and thinkers at Bellingham Unitarian Fellowship (BUF). Thanks to Shasta Pettijohn and the BUF Coffee House team. Thanks to Rev. Tessie Mandeville and Jeff Packer for their presence of mind and open hearts, and for their hospice work at PeaceHealth St. Joseph Medical Center. Thanks to Bellingham Technical College and Whatcom Community College. Additional thanks to the Whatcom Community College Library and Community and Continuing Education staff.

Thanks and admiration to Duke Ashrafuzzaman, Ashok Bhargava and Bernice Lever. Thanks to The Tagore Festival; Writers International Network; World Poetry of Canada; the Vine Deloria Symposium; SwilKanim and the leaders and Elders of Lummi Nation.

Thanks to Village Books. Day in and day out they provide literature, food, programs, and a community spirit that nourishes even the loneliest among us. Thanks to The Public Market and Film Is Truth for their generosity, smiles, and the space to rehearse.

Thanks and gratitude to you, Dear Readers. Proceeds of every book will go to Lummi Youth Academy, a 24-bed residential dormitory for Native youth ages 12-18. According to Amy Shimek, Academic Team Supervisor, "In the past 10 years Lummi Youth Academy has supported 171 at-risk Native youth by developing their life skills, achievements, academics and health care."

With appreciation, Betty Scott

Dear Readers,

For decades people in the United States have asked: *Can poetry matter?* thanks greatly to the insights and observations of author, critic and California poet laureate Dana Gioia. For many whose values or interests are defined by the marketplace, the answer is a simple "no." For me *Can poetry matter?* suggests political and social questions equivalent to asking: *does being a father or mother matter? Do grandparents and children matter? Does Mother Nature and the land we walk on matter?* For many, poetry becomes the landscape of our living.

Unfortunately, with little respect for the planet's survival, humans have warred against each other and slaughtered sentient beings. These actions pull poets and readers alike toward the call of ancestors, toward a curiosity about origins, the mystery of our family-tree stories. I was called quite unexpectedly as I sat in a municipal court room. Six jurors were selected that day. I was not one of them. Yet everything about that morning said: *Pay Attention; Full Attention; Surrender To What Is Happening Here.*

My juror number was my birth date and month. The stranger beside me was attractive and friendly. As we waited for jury selection to begin, we whispered like children swapping secret family stories. He told me a move to the segregated South when he was seven invoked in him his moral outrage. In college, he marched against the Vietnam War in Washington, D.C., as our military stood on rooftops with guns aimed at the marchers. A professor of religious studies now, he turned back to his Bible. I opened up a newspaper. Suddenly I was reading of a dear friend's death. In the courtroom, waiting for lawyers to return, I grieved. The silence of those around me felt stiff, dutiful and irreverent.

The court case involved a homeless man who had disturbed the library's silence and threatened the head librarian. Suddenly, my most cherished values were pitted against each other.

As an educator, librarians have long been my unsung heroes. As a member of a family with chronic illnesses, and as a support person for those who lose loved ones to suicide, my stomach ached. Still today, as then, our culture provides little practical support, nor sustained training for those who are ill, living with traumas, struggling to earn a living. Today, as then, I want to protect librarians and people with chronic illnesses before that leads to homelessness. When I was dismissed from my civic duty that day, I walked the lonely streets to my locked car. It was time to reckon with: *What use am I?*

So began two tumultuous years. I lost funding for my job, not just any job, but what I considered my life's work. I lost friendships associated with that work. Inexplicably with my heart broken open, I put myself into the hands of words. Like fingers, they stroked and prodded. I wrote down poems that called to me, guided me through grief, loss, betrayal and confusion. I felt their rhythms, sounds, images, meanings, and energy. I discovered syllables are the electro-chemical molecules of the spirit. They call us to witness and to heal.

During this time, I also received several synchronistic calls from others; friends from long ago when I needed to hear their voices. One morning the phone rang and I heard: "This is your cousin, Betsy. Did you know we had a cousin named Michael? He died yesterday. Age 49. How come our parents never told us about him?"

Mystery is the optimist's word for confusion. As a poet, I write from within the snowstorm of my external and internal worlds. I listen. Words shower down like snowflakes. I shovel. A poem comes together and falls apart. I shovel on. My battered ego eventually, painfully, asks the poem what it wants to be. Before bedtime, I read over the day's attempts. When I'm tired, they don't make sense. I leave the poems alone until morning. At first waking, I listen and shovel until in spirit's time, each poem shapes itself syllable by syllable, word by word.

I love being of use to poetry. When north winds chill, when snowflakes fall, when external and internal worlds tremor, when love and grief cover my feet and climb to my knees, then poems summon me to clear a path lit by the sun, moon and stars. I've walked along my winding trail for many years now. It's been humbling. I've nurtured and raised many poems; in turn, they have raised me.

Through our collaboration, publisher Doug Johnson, artist Alfredo Arreguín, musician JP Falcon Grady and I think you'll find nurturing words here, with melodies and images that echo your family stories.

When asked: "does poetry matter?" we hope you'll nod, smile, hug a parent or a child with renewed compassion and desire to protect your future generations. We believe as the bell tolls, now is the moment to listen with protective compassion to species, seas, trees and humanity on Earth.

With Best Wishes,

Betty Scott
Bellingham, Washington

Table of Contents

Magnetics:

Our Town excerpt	1
Generous Universe	3
Tree Reflections	4
Central Heating	5
Keeping House	6
Great to Be I	8
Great to Be II	9
A Courtroom And A Waterfall	10
Dear Lonely Muse,	13
Betty Goes To Yoga	14
Love Is A Many Splintered Thing	15
Raising A Poet	16
Flirting At The Neighborhood Bakery	17
As I Wake From A Dream	19
Dear Fred,	20
After Words I	22
After Words II	25
Savings	26
First Steps	28
After His Sister Dies	32
Thirty-Six Lines In Defense Of Clutter	34
The Playground	36
Roots And Seeds	37
May Peace Become Us	38

Dark Matter(s):
    Triad   41
    The Guarded Wound   41
Life Braids   43
My Dog Barks   44
Paying Homage I   45
Between Capricorn And Cancer   46
My Middle Finger   48
Dear Cake And Bake,   50
Husbandry   51
ode to butter   57
Beyond My Wrists   59
On The Day I Prayed To Mother Mary   60
The Foghorn   61
A Poet Prays For Peace   63

Renewable Energies:
    Release   65
    Refusing Silence   65

After Words Meditation   67
Portals   68
Ducks Fly   69
What Sarah Couldn't Say To Abraham   70
In God He Trusts; In Sleep He Trysts With Death   72
Dry Creek Beds And Streams   73
The Day After Eighty-Two Years Beyond   78
Megaphone Song   79
Simply Simplify   81
Paying Homage II   84
one day i was feeling oppressed and said right out loud   85
Waking Spirit   87
He Sails Us To Shore   88

Demonstrations	89
An Earth Year Blessing	92
Canoe Journey Moon	93
Bless Thee	94
Metamorphosis	95
I Woke One Morning	97
Beneath February's Slivered Moon	100
Central Healing	101
A Northwest Winter's Dream	104
The Poet's Legacy	105
Notes to the Poems	107
About the Author	111

Magnetics

From *Our Town*
Emily*: Oh earth, you're too wonderful*
for anyone to realize you.
Do any human beings realize life
while they live it?
Every, every minute?

Stage Manager:
No. Saints and poets, maybe.
They do some.

—Thornton Wilder

Generous Universe

On a walk
as blue jays squawk
I find a wad of money

and in a crack
between cement blocks
a purple and white pansy.

Tree Reflections

Winter tree
your shadow
is a blackened
crucifix

your morning
wind dance
a silent
swaying

Christmas hologram
your leafless
limbs are
wise men

bearing gifts
of despair
joy and mystery
your branches

upturned
I recall
beloved arms
a sleeping baby.

Central Heating

In my dream I'm teaching a troubled classroom.
It's mid-quarter, no grades recorded.

I wake to a February day beneath the sliver
of a new moon.

I slide to work on icy roads
and scribble out this formula:

Homework
Life sparks Sorrow's circuits:

Grief-Anger-Fear (GAF)
+ Yesterdays, Today, Tomorrows (YsDTOs)
+ 3x Static between Thoughts (STbTHs)
- Silent Meditations through Time (SHMEtT)
+ and – Love (L) = Life's Test (LT).

GAF + YsDTOs + 3x(STbTHs) – SHMEtT + and – L = LT

Solve for earth and self.

Keeping House

in my father's house
i kill daddy long legs
fragile   with feelers

they lurk in the corners
in the shadows   on walls
and shower stalls

when i'm around
they dangle and scurry
for safe ground

in my father's house
those he loves   he blames
as often as his moods change

his family   luggage to him
to stuff with his belongings
and empty at his whim

even at eighty
loneliness   betrays him
one day my father locks

his front door and tells
his mexican cleaning lady
it's time to sleep with him

i've got money
my father says
i'll pay you

now when i shower
i lock the bathroom door
where the daddy long legs live

in the corners and shadows
dangling ever too close
i kill daddy long legs

do you judge me
tell me
wouldn't you do the same?

Great To Be I

At a gathering of writers
a professor said to me:
"Poets are different
from other people."

I rummaged
through my brain
then ruefully replied
"I don't think so."

He repeated his decree
and as I slept that night
I proved myself
a prime example

for I woke up
awed and spoke
out loud, "I touched
the life force of a tree,"

and
I wrote
that down
thoughtfully.

Great To Be II

For Cindy

After the student performs her songs of home
the professors on her right and left lean in
and decree, as though to console her soul:
"Pianists are a unique specie."

"Yes, it's true," they repeat, as they are trained
to clarify: "This term you will identify,
categorize, research and support the academic
premise that pianists are distinctly different."

She replies with a nod and a quiet "I see,"
that leads her through *Where do I belong?*
a fretful sleep and flat-footed dreams
until she returns to the Lakota Medicine Wheel

to play her pine, birch and cedar songs,
and when her fingers strike the keys
yes, it's great to be and wake up *awed*
under Lummi Island's Academy of Trees.

A Courtroom And A Waterfall

I.

Such an ordinary day I assumed
though I sat on a bench in a courtroom
among strangers, dutiful and wooden

waiting for attorneys to return.
Some of us would be chosen
to judge a homeless man

jittery, in an ill-fitting suit
hair combed and gelled into place;
he'd yelled obscenities in a library

angered and threatened the librarian.
She called the police;
they cuffed and took him away.

II.

You sat beside me, a scholar
with a weathered backpack
and dog-eared Bible as Lit. text.

Our whispers broke the room's silence.

You spoke of a Southern childhood,
cultural cruelties, segregated fountains
and pools. You were seven, you said,

when moral outrage over took you.
In college, as soldiers fought in Vietnam,
you marched through D.C. streets

against city cops and barricades,
military on roof-tops,
rifles cocked, aimed at marchers below.

You returned to your Bible.
I opened a newspaper.
In the black print

of daily news, I read
of a dear friend's
death.

III.

It's a challenge to clarify
what happened next.
Beside me, you remained

eager and present.
Not the moment to tell you
about Calene.

Attorneys returned, my spirit
plummeted and emerged
and through you I felt a jolt

of joy, then, as if riding
a waterfall, I plunged
into green glacial waters

beneath sadness and joy
where grief and love
co-exist.

IV.

I learned that day a jury
hasn't much to say to those
who churn in the deepest pools

of uncertainty where the ill
and the well keep faith.
I reached toward you,

a scholar with a Bible,
and like joy and sorrow
you left without good-bye.

V.

Grief and joy in a free-
spirit moment, my soul-hold.
Since then I've trawled for love

in a snow melt of memories
nearly drowned in a stream
of poems. Did I dive

into the grace of clear waters
or jump, feet scrambling, splashing
between rocks, churning up mud?

I don't recall climbing out, water dripping
off the ends of my hair, the cuffs of my jeans,
dirt clinging to my ankles and between my toes.

Please tell me, Calene, when your spirit
broke free from your sick body
did you find yourself safely home?

Dear Lonely Muse,

how does the spirit
stay alive, seduced
unrealized?

Betty Goes To Yoga

He stood sentry on an island
between asphalt traffic lanes.

He had a chiseled nose and chin
his hair shoulder length.

In each hand, barbell bags
of groceries hung.

To be quite clear as I drove by
I imagined us and ecstasized.

But now on my yoga mat
I stretch

breathe out and realize
breathe in

I am old enough
breathe out

to be his mother.
Some say:

gasp in, his
grandmother.

Love Is A Many Splintered Thing

Artist's Love

When we stare
Into the deepest eyes of intimacy

Discipline and commitment
Shine back.

Family Love

When we grieve and love
Our bodies tune and hum

To ancient rhythms of home.

Sacred Love

When we dare open
The mouth of love

We taste grief before joy.

Raising A Poet

"Walk; Don't Run," cannot be translated by Liberty Rose's twelve-year-old feet. They've grown wide in the sand beside the sea. At a crosswalk when the light turns green, Liberty Rose outpaces the beat of her mother's high heels. She skips through the shadows and light on a galloping pony, passing an old lady, bent like a twig. The elder spits out: "Comb your hair." Mother agrees; she steers Liberty Rose and her curly knots for two downtown blocks. At the beauty school, Liberty Rose is restrained in a chair that rides up and down. She wiggles beneath a plastic cape, tied behind her neck, heavy on her arms, until her body is tucked in like a braided mane.

Valerie labors to comb Liberty's curls out. She calls to Amber and then to Crystal. All three tug and pull. To stop her tears from flowing, Liberty wills her eyes shut. Eventually they wash and tame Liberty's knots. Valerie cuts, dries, straightens and styles. She lowers the chair. She wraps Liberty's fingers around the handle of a mirror and turns Liberty Rose around.

"That's much better," Mother smiles. Valerie bends, whispers into Liberty's ear. "Look through this mirror to the mirror behind you, and you'll see the back of your head."

Liberty Rose raises her eyes. Beyond her face framed in a hand-held mirror, beyond her styled and sprayed waves of hair, a pony grazes in a field of grass, its tail switching and flicking at flies. Then like a mare that's learned the code, Liberty Rose smiles slightly, nods, and shakes her mane.

Flirting At The Neighborhood Bakery

I don't know what I want yet, he says
to the woman behind the glass case,

his words defying the authority
of his frontal stance before her

morning glory muffins, cinnamon twists,
strawberry and cream cheese sweet rolls.

She replies: *That's the way with people
these days. We don't know what we want.*

He laughs. She laughs. Years strip off them
easily, the way orange rinds peel off.

Her brown eyes widen. No longer a woman in polyester,
she dances in a velvet skirt and laced apron,

earrings swaying in the embrace
and swing of her blue-eyed lover.

He leans way back in his boots,
his jean-clad thighs thrust forward.

I'll take a latte and a bran muffin, he says.
May I warm the muffin, she asks.

He waits, pacing the length of the display case,
but facing her, his energy to her.

She puts a lid on the latte, slips
his muffin into a sack.

They move to the cash register. She rings up
the purchases, overcharges him, laughs,

rings him up again. His hand knocks the stem
of a spoon in a dish of shredded chocolate.

The spoon clangs to the floor. Around his boots,
bittersweet bits of chocolate scatter. He blushes,

she blushes, both caught doing something delicious.

As I Wake From A Dream

I say to no one but myself:
"Let's start the world,"
as if the world had vanished
while I slept.

As if the universe has said:
We're tired of our orbits;
you take over for a while.
What's your plan?

As if Science, Technology
and Hollywood can
turn mosquitoes into planets
and lice into stars.

As if thirst and tears
and mourning breaths can
cross Earth's deserts, roll
down mountains and laugh.

Dear Fred,

When Germany invaded Czechoslovakia,
You joined freedom fighters saying:
Every man and woman must stand up
For what they believe. Shot, captured,

Interrogated and tortured, you maintained:
Every man and woman must stand up
For what they believe. Five hell years
Later you were freed. Beyond Buchenwald,

Starved and sick, you crossed the ocean in 1946
To bring sixty orphans from Germany to the U.S.
Along the way, you taught the children
To stand up for what they believe.

Years later, you were quoted: *those kids saved me.*
Through your 70s and 80s, you served the elderly,
Fought for those with mental disease,
Urged our region to stand for peoples' needs.

Now, I think of you with immortals
Beside the writer Jean Webster, debating the tyranny
Of pain brought on by behaviors no generation escapes:
Hatred, betrayal, greed – embedded in our anatomy.

While time, cultures and class kept you two apart
I imagine your souls now woven, singing
For creativity, for those in poverty
For people quieted with disabilities

Singing for women, children, the elderly
For acceptance of love in sexuality
An army of souls linked in spirit
Singing their heavenly songs

For the rights of immigrants to get along
Singing for health care for every one
Singing for our water, air and trees
Singing for our community's rights and needs.

After Words I

That last time we saw each other you stood
in stony triumph at Trader Joe's

between rows of meat and cartons of milk,
ninety-two years frail in a neck brace

moments after being released from the hospital
for pneumonia and broken vertebrae.

"Give me a sign," I said, "when you pass on."
You volleyed back: "I don't believe in an afterlife,"

yet with me, you talked possibilities
before we hugged good-bye.

Months later, on the day you died—
a blink in astral time—I received the sign,

where else but at Trader Joe's.
I thought I was after a bargain

in what Homer called "liquid gold" and stood
before row after row of green, brown and amber

bottles of olive oil. Beside me a stranger,
her hair straight brown, ending at her chin,

her shirt tucked in: "I'm looking for olive oil,"
she said, "to use on my face. My friend's beauty

secret to ward off wrinkles.
She's fifty-five. Barely looks thirty."

We talked and laughed like old friends,
this stranger and me, until she revealed

"I see things in black and white.
I work with numbers. Numbers don't lie."

I volleyed back: "People use numbers
to prove anything they want."

"That's my point," she said. "People lie.
Numbers are right or wrong. Black or white.

I like numbers. I don't like people." She smiled affably
unaware of her impact as she repeated the formula

you fought against, the sum and total, those same words spoken
to me when my work hours were cut that week.

Dear Mentor, at home I unpacked that dark bottle
of olive oil. A lonely breath later the phone rang.

I was told you'd died. No wonder I'm intrigued
with olives, oil, and trees.

Olive trees, millions of years old, are sacred pillars
of ancient societies. Hallowed drops of oil

seeped into the bones of dead saints and martyrs
through holes in their tombs.

I trust you'd understand my nightly ritual, a few drops
of olive oil on my face and hands to defend against decay.

Dear Pillar, as I pay homage to you
and to your afterlife, I wonder

Where are you dear friend?
Ancient as ashes, I reason
And as integral as olive trees.

After Words II

when I wake
silence hides in the shadows
of gossip and pain.

Savings

My dachshund, Mona Lisa,
understands rhythms,
the proper pace for living.
She dwells nose to tail, curled in sleep.

Mona's a senior citizen now
and I am grateful for time with her
to learn that food matters in equal
measure to naps. And that's not all.

When I dress and put on make-up
she yelps in protest: *Don't leave me!*
She cocks her head
to emphasize my offense.

We are leashed to exercise
by 4 p.m. each day.
That's not negotiable
unless it rains.

Be attentive, she counsels.
*Watch out for birds, cats,
and humans. Make your bed
of peace and sleep in it.*

*Scratch what itches,
that's a given. Most of all,
define yourself properly,
as I see you.*

Lately, it is here
I feel her praise.
*Finally you have
noticed*, she tells me:

*I am a lap dog; you
are my lap. Your work
and destiny? To sit for hours
contentedly with me.*

She speaks through silence
with the wisdom of a Zen master:
*You have so much to learn.
Don't make me bark at you again.*

So I tell her
being unemployed
is a blessing.
I've opened

a savings account
to bank my emotions
and prepare for the losses
a job will bring.

First Steps

1.
As a gardener
I'm contented
to walk the bay
into the wind

my mantra:
*who am I
to kill
what lives.*

The Jains
of India
believe souls
transmigrate;
they protect
plants, birds
even insects.

Avoiding
yard duty
is easy
for me
through winter.

In early spring
I enjoy
the last
sweet taste
of denial

until Northwest grass
grows from ankles
to knees
to entanglements.

Then I take
that first step
beneath denial
to grapple with
life and death.

2.
It begins
with labor pains
the first
two-hour mow,

who lives
who dies
who grows
what can I
neglect?

Even so
these first
steps down
this garden path
are relatively easy.

It's turning back
that weighs
most heavily.

For once I've got
dirt on my hands
I turn against
dandelions.

3.
Dandelions are
international
travelers.
In France, they
are called
pissenlit,

which means
urinate in bed
a bow to
their diuretic
properties.

Italians may refer
to them as
dog pisses
for their
pavement
flourishings.

Nations name them
for their milky
sweetness
their buttery color
or common status.

The *blowing flower*
their seeds disperse
in the wind
the carrier
of life
and death.

So I ask:
in our gardens
with dirt
under our nails
when will we
turn back?

After His Sister Dies

1.

The dead
tell us:

insights
      have
           no
                      deadlines

2.

The dead
tell us:

actions that spring
from in-sights
            have
                no
                      dead – lines

3.

The dead
tell us:

in-sights have
no dead-lines
                      us
                need
          you
                need
                      us

4.

The dead say:
listen closely

hear us
whisper

you need not
be hostages
to grief

you may
stop
bashing

your
self
and us

you may
stop
sacrificing

      any
           time
                now

                        would
                  you
  ? we   wish
                  you
                        would

Thirty-six Lines In Defense Of Clutter

I was a newlywed with a mother-
in-law whose house was spotless and white-gloved
where carpet remnants brightened her garage,
so in my house I tried for that mirage
dutifully with faith for a year or three
until life retrained me, and I made peace
with clutter, stuff in boxes, closed with tape,
my house a changeling for children and pets,
until yoga instructors and coaches
defined procrastination, advised us
to clean up clutter from homes, bodies, souls,
drawer by drawer, breath by breath where voices pull
against hearts locked to uninvited guests,
and there my former mother-in-law sits
not in my life, yet beside me, tempered
as a hammer that knocks the stakes of time,
returning me to Christmas Eves, bearing
boxes of unwanted toys for "her boys"
(gifts for me each year the same: an apron
and two long-sleeved, floor-length flannel nightgowns)
ignoring the joys of her granddaughter,
refusing to eat my roasted turkey
saying: "We stopped for barbeque and prawns,"
my heart and hands sinking beneath soap suds
where I learned to breathe and procrastinate
and though my kids refuse to ruminate,
I arm myself with rickety boxes
and fight dust mites, rats and flooding waters,
ripping that duct tape, packing and storing
their scrawlings beside ancestral drawings,
penciled tallies wrapped in faded tissues,
voices that slumber on planks nailed to walls

to speak when kids return to this garage,
do the job passed down like a coat of arms
to relive and reclaim their papered coins
as faithful as silver and drafts of poems.

The Playground

In writing it's a well-known fact:
letters are lizards with legs and tails
syllables bite like alligator teeth
words blossom like magnolia trees.

It's no lie: in swamps and fields, the wind strokes
and ripples the tiniest wild flower
that under the light of a microscope
lives as complex as an orchid or rose.

It's a fact: the cells of grasses and leaves
resemble living streams and arteries.
In marshes, hollow reeds are fiddle strings
that shadow the shallows and hallowed-winged.

It's the truth: people swarm, sip, and worship
our playgrounds during festival seasons
as the heirs to brass notes float, fall, and rise
beneath the gumbo of moon and moonshine.

While the infinite and miniscule breed
while lizards, swamps and birds battle to breathe
the heated U.S. is rooted and twined
to nature's rhythms and rhymes. Who rests?

Roots And Seeds

I have come to learn of moments that return

just as

after a fight	reason	returns	to roost
after fires burn	ashes	drift	to earth
after bells chime	silence	vibrates	in kind
after flight	geese	nest	with their young
after picking cotton	yarn	blankets	us with warmth
after a tree harvest	pages	rustle	in volumes on shelves

just as

offerings from blossoms to kumquats to us become sweet marmalade.

I have come to learn the signals

how   cell roots   and seeds   grow   to connect   and   interweave
how   electrical   impulses   inward and   out   pulse and
                                                                                                   repeat

how the micro and infinite intertwine and center for nourishment.

I have come to learn of eventualities

death   as   a   be-coming   and   yet

I have come to pray

you and I, surviving beings, will resolve the us of us.

May Peace Become Us

> *Honoring and acknowledging Lhaq'temish Traditional Territories*
> *since time immemorial Lhaq'temish, "the People"*
> *have lived in these territories*
> *—Lummi Nation*

Through the sword of history
and the pen of greed

humanity destroys diversity
oceans dry up, species starve

yet come with me to the dance studio
not to indulge, not even in remorse

but to return to the ballet barre
the underbelly that feeds

precision and technique
until well-practiced in discipline

through the facts of history
we realize at home on Earth

that this is the moment
a sentence becomes an outstretched arm and leg

fingers poised, toes pointed
eyes focused, head erect

and in the practice of peace
through grace and beauty, light and music

the sentence becomes the weight of the world
and the path to Earth's bio-sanctuary …

Dark Matter(s)

Triad

These be
three silent things:
The falling snow…the hour
Before the dawn…the mouth of one
Just dead

—Adelaide Crapsey

The Guarded Wound

*If it
Were lighter touch
Than petal of flower resting
On grass, oh still too heavy it were,
Too heavy!*

—Adelaide Crapsey

Life Braids

love that unites us
also unties us

when we perceive
or believe

in a small i
on the loose …

My Dog Barks

She's an old lady now
our silent talks and walks numbered.
Soon I will miss her long stretches
the arc and arch of her spine

her struts to the back door, tail up
curled nails against sliding glass
black nose pointed toward grass
her return, the scrape and scamper

and later, her warm body
against the middle of the night
even her littering rights.
Exigencies of living–with the art

of her in starts and stops
her leash and release of me.

Paying Homage I

I kneel outside my dining room
Pull dandelions from the soil
Above my dachshund's bones

Behind me, a crow heralds
From the crown of a Douglas fir
Its caw reigning down as I work

I find two empty peanut shells
Grieve for those cast aside
Can't air betrayals or forgive The

Boss, so I dust off and cradle
These shells, their grit and dirt
Return them to the earth

Between Capricorn And Cancer

In the beginning
of the Drought Era
a woman stands in the shade

of a well. She will raise
a bucket and carry it,
careful to save every drop

for her family
should she stumble
over fallen kumquats

rotting on parched ground.
On their veranda
she will hold the bucket

in both hands and with
a quick lift and tilt
water will scatter

into a porcelain bowl
that sits on a three-legged stool.
She will dip her hands

in prayer, lift drops
to her lips and wipe
a tear for her son

a teen entering
that torrid zone and for
her younger daughter too.

On this day before others
in the house rise
soldiers will order the woman

to reach beneath the seat
of the stool for a key
hidden there, though

the lockbox that belongs
to the key will no longer
shield her family.

On this day
beyond prayers
she will mourn

May my children
reflect,
yield like water.

My Middle Finger

Braided between my opposable
thumb and dainty pinkie, my
middle finger, all three inches

its half-moon nail neatly
trimmed, has never been
polished in purple, rarely

polished at all except
with scorn's mournful
back trails to the sword's

indifference, especially before
elections, those spitty-spat
days when my middle

finger steadies a pen
dips itself in
political cans of blood

becomes a switch-blade
flicks and flings and scatters
drops of red, wipes itself clean

but not before my middle
finger becomes an elevator
ascending to the penthouse floor

its signature a clear-cut above
all those opposable thumbs and
dainty pinkies below, my middle

finger, the mightiest digit
of all, a perch for bears'
and black birds' claws.

Dear Cake And Bake,

Tell me about angel-food kittens
with their sour cream paws
and eyes of blue-green mints.

Tell me about sugar asters,
poems I threw in the trash
shattered shards of sugar glass.

Tell me about Marlon Brando's
sugared fists. Fame's burst of taste
still scintillates even the lips of saints.

Tell me about Mother Teresa
kneeling nonetheless
to pray and soothe with wafers.

Tell me about writer's cramp, waxy
tongues, cranial nerves, bursts of sorrow.
Tell me, Supreme Cake and Bake,

how do placated, half-baked turtles,
necks outstretched, ingesting
plastic shards, survive?

Husbandry

I. Decades Before The Public Is Aware of Global Warming:

There she is: home from work and in the kitchen
a single mother with three school-age kids
and no relatives close by.

She pours tomato sauce into a pan.
A pot of water for noodles steams on the stove.
After she puts her children to bed

she must find a babysitter for her sick child
and stay up past midnight to prepare
power point slides, then leave at 8 a.m. to play her role

as a speaker at a state-wide gathering of teachers
who have come to learn about fostering
better business communications.

After she speaks she'll rush to her college
to teach two classes back to back.
She'll speed home to ease her guilt

for leaving her daughter feverish
on the couch, a child who longs for
her Daddy, ill and missing-from-action.

She stirs the tomato sauce bubbling on the stove
turns off the heat under the kettle of boiling water
and carries noodles to the sink, heavy in her arms.

She holds a glass lid with one hand and tilts the pot
careful not to dump the noodles out. The sink clogs.
Hot water rises and steam fogs her glasses.

She swears and runs to the bathroom
grabs a plunger, pushes and pumps
until the cloudy water drains out.

Her oldest son yells from his room
"What's that sound?" Her youngest, playing
with blocks beside his sister, yells back:

"That's Mommy making dinner."
Her chapped hands itch; her face
turns red; a sob boils up.

For a moment she's so overcome
she wipes her tears and prays:
Dear God, please help.

Soon the door bell rings, a loud
Short, *short, short … Short, short, short.*
The thumbprint sounds of her dear friend

a WWII veteran, radio broadcaster,
twenty-years older than she.
He says: *I felt a need to drop by.*

He's finished his supper
and has driven a dozen miles.
He wears dirty coveralls, a thin coat

and stands in the shadow of her porch
eager to come inside. *Oh my,* she realizes
My friend's been sent by God.

II.   *Years Before Learning the Ice Caps Have Melted:*

Her friend refers to himself
as "something like a husband."
One day he arrives unannounced, as usual.

She is listening to the radio.
He comes into her kitchen and with the ease
of an expert turns the dial to a station he prefers.

Resentments boil up.
How could he feel so entitled?
She is struck dumb and unsettled

by an anger that could melt an iceberg.
Hard for her to believe that something
so ordinary could cause this cellular shift.

She drifts with her thoughts
blames and makes excuses for him
imagines herself as an angel

lying on her back, waving
her arms in the snow
as though whatever unsettles her

could be blessed by wings of silence.
She hides for weeks in the shadows
of her conflict, crusty as ice, as if she prizes

the protection from feelings above all else
as if their friendship has not shifted
electrified by the static of words they leave unsaid.

*III.   Today as Exxon Mobil Spreads Uncertainty About Extinction,
Monsanto's Products Flourish, and the Planet Loses Biodiversity
at an Unprecedented Rate:*

She wonders: what will the earth record?
Will it be more war and retribution
the cry and shuffle of refugees' feet

or, on the brink of human extinction
peoples' world-wide prayers for peace?
Decades ago, gobbled up

inside the guts of education and health
the institutions people turn to for help
she witnessed political and fiscal feeding frenzies.

She still prays whenever CEOs, politicians
or publishers, blind to earth's
over-fished and polluted waters

hunt like sharks or like angler fish
their glowing lights, razor-sharp teeth
and massive mouths open wide

while orcas in their family pods
click, whistle and call, traveling thousands
of bootlegged miles beside our manmade trawlers.

Still, she watches for cellular shifts
for those in power to glide
like ice angels through upstream

channels of remorse
to align at last, globally,
with the husbandry of earth.

Her longtime friend
does not agree
with all the fuss

over trains, and coal
and oil. *Progress,*
he says: *technology and jobs.*

Yet she reminds him
of that night
twenty years ago

how the next day he returns
to stay with her sick child
so she can get to work.

Before she reaches
the conference room's podium
wind and rain soak her hair

but she makes it, and on time—
she rushes to college, teaches
two classes, returns home frazzled.

There, under the light of a lamp
her daughter reads a book
a glass of water in arm's reach.

Mom, she says, *he sings! Show her.*
Sing for my Mom. He laughs
I will. But first, he puts down his pencil

hands the child a cartoon
a caricature of an old man
teaching a girl to fish.

"Trout tonight
with lemon and butter,"
he sings in his baritone.

ode to butter

cruelty—our history—
spreads, and that's
the jam we're in...

on taste buds
butter is better
than bitter

on buds of societal tastes
butter is better
than margarine

and being bitter-free inside
the tribe is better
than being marginalized

trouble is: during winter times
grief talks, clogs the heart
pools like fat beneath the skin

and in the mean times
opinion talks, clogs the brain
stalls oxygen throughout our veins

still, butter
is better
than bitter

so women bring on the butter
biscuits and gravy
cookies dipped in butter cream

trouble is: care givers
have been told   *Your stories
don't matter politically—*

*not brief enough
cut them to the bone
use reason ... critical thinking....*

trouble is: through winter times
mean times, history's taught us
batter is better with butter

so for logic's sake and for love
women spread themselves thin
golden smooth and creamy

trouble is: since Mother Mary
first Christmas maker
gifted care taker

mothers more or less
have been told
Oh hush, Big Child

*don't disturb
denial...*
trouble is

cruelty—our history—
spreads, and that's
the jam we're in...

Beyond My Wrists

A doe and two fawns graze in my yard as I
head out for an afternoon walk. Two blocks away
three black-tailed bucks stare me down, their ears swivel
toward me, their eyes liquid brown. A car passes by.
Their ears swivel back.
                        As schools are built, more herds
take to roads, vacuum-sealed, as we are, in pickle-
jar streets within the vinegar brine of urbanized time.
If God would wave his wand of grace over us

if we'd make holy all mothers and children displaced …
This morning when I opened my dining room drapes
a spotted fawn, closed in, was nuzzling beneath
its mother's back legs, its triangular muzzle upturned.
Imagine godly love in the thirst of a kid
that drinks, as it did, from its maternal fountain of piss.

On The Day I Prayed To Mother Mary

To some it's crazy, this solace from pain
Found simply beneath a lady bug's wings
Yet after months of illness, grief and nerves
I sank to my knees and prayed to Mother
Mary. In fear, I drove to the doctor
And on my way, a lady bug hovered
So regal in her coat of black and red.
She landed on my windshield and folded
Her wings, holding still for a mile or more
As though she were the one to guide the car.
When I slowed to park, she rose from her glass
Perch, waved her wings and flew away, her task
Now done. Such relief traveled through my veins
I embodied a living faith with wings.

The Foghorn

After I chewed and swallowed my most vulnerable self
with the last morsel of salad greens, dressed
in sweet rice vinegar and virgin olive oil, I was still hungry
for a turkey and melted cheese on toast, so I
chewed and swallowed that too   And smiled

By 3 a.m. I woke from a dreamless sleep
while my most vulnerable self traveled
down my esophagus and met my raw stomach lining
which signaled my electrical energy system
to make its sweep in a search and vacuum mission
gathering foreign particles and toxins
from the maze of my small and large intestines
which signaled my muscles to contract

and the next thing I know, I am belching
and burping and belching my most vulnerable self
releasing her, yet again, through my throat
where the Thou Shalt Nots and the Ten
Commandments of my Soul are reduced
to a single mouth, lips parting
giving birth to a fatherless, motherless
universal self, species unknown, spinning
in air and ether until its spores nest

once again … and once again …
every day is Groundhog Day
potentially holy… asking … *what should I do now?*

*Will I throw the venerable, vulnerable ones
into the photon nuclear accelerators
of artificial intelligence where cellular
demolishing, particles of being, cells of body-less
Self belong to a gossiping galaxy?   Or*

*Will I sit in Buddha nature with loving kindness
cuddle, warm, and resonate with the energies
inside vulnerabilities to bring abilities ... to light?*

A Poet Prays For Peace

> *I am so small*
> *I can barely be seen:*
> *How can this great love be inside me?*
> *Look at your eyes. They're small*
> *But they see enormous things.*
> —Rumi

Dear Lord,
greed blossoms in
people of many hues
and our cruelties breed disdain
for precious living things

we label, blame, and call
compassion … co-dependency
war against each other
spit on Mother
Nature

disperse
war refugees
like dandelion seeds
and even though through centuries
most nations claim to be

the best above the rest
please lead us forward, Lord, at last
so that we know we're in
each other's hands
to live

off each
other's interests
like a trust, until seeds
of love, peace and empathy sprout
in us, then please cradle

us, till us, Dear Lord, grow
awareness in us and bring our
orphans home, bring them home
Lord, please, with us
be home …

Renewable Energies

Release

With swift
Great sweep of her
Magnificent arm my pain
Clanged back the doors that shut my soul
From life.

—Adelaide Crapsey

From Refusing Silence

There are messages to send.
Gatherings and songs.
Because we need
to insist. Else what are we
for? What use
are we?

—Tess Gallagher
in Amplitude and Midnight Lantern

After Words Meditation

In the wake
of black and white
hatred rising

social justice out-
shadowed by slogans and lies
most nights I sit

with a plate of olives
tangy black ones, buttery
Castelvetrano greens

and hold words close
believing in poems as prisms
that shine with light

Portals

At this threshold
when our thoughts
are continents apart

I listen for footsteps
and within the silence
between each footfall

I imagine love
a stained-glass window
fractured selves sustained

side-by-side
dual light-streams
in a Galilee porch.

Ducks Fly

For Carol

With ninety-year-old eyes full of spirit,
Carol hunts for her keys, cell phone, glasses
and the batteries to her hearing aid.
Before we start out, she searches nine pockets

in her over-stuffed purse, strewn with dollars
and bills she meant to mail, her fingers guided
by thoughts that grasp for her husband
of sixty-eight years who died in January

and for her children and grandchildren who moved away.
Buckled up, we head out in heavy traffic.
A mallard appears, wings outstretched, mottled brown
white belly feathers, long neck and beak … driving toward Carol

toward broken wings, a shattered windshield, glass blasting
against thin layers of aged skin. And so in honking traffic
I brake. An eye-inch away, the mallard lifts
and with grace of flight and wit, Carol replies:

To duck or not to duck; that is the question.
You should write a poem. What rhymes with duck?
Now, until life us do part, through losses that suck,
we laugh and say: *when life ducks us, just duck.*

What Sarah Couldn't Say To Abraham

I'd like you
to come with me.

Under the sandpaper sun
we'll be brown and tender.

We'll sit under a magenta umbrella
and watch the waves of the bay

wash over the islands
hazy and tree-green.

Yet you bring finely-tuned eyes and ears
and warm up on a black and white keyboard

to play judgmental sonatas.
I won't be your pedals today.

Wine will make you happy
that's what you'll say

but when the wine is served
it will be too sweet.

For a moment, I may forget
who I am. But don't expect

me to wear a nun's habit
placed as I am in another court.

Your eyes won't see this
but I turn and flash my naked back

to you.

In God He Trusts; In Sleep He Trysts With Death

A dark crow squawks outside his bay window
As I enter Dad's house this lonely day.
He lies so still, his face a worn pillow.

In his silent home, belongings echo.
"I'm here, Dad," I call from the entry way.
A dark crow squawks outside his bay window.

In his room, silence moans without sorrow.
I reach for his shoulder, call out his name.
He sleeps so still, his face a worn pillow.

I touch his lips and nose to see breath flow.
Must you be so blissful, I dare not say.
A dark crow squawks outside his bay window.

"I'm a great sleeper now," he wakes and boasts
"Practicing for the big sleep … on its way."
He lies so still, his face a worn pillow.

Yet I've seen inside the beak of a crow
Blood red and cawing love's longings and pain.
A dark crow squawks outside his bay window.
He lies so still, his face a worn pillow.

Dry Creek Beds And Streams

1.
When Dad was eighty-nine
he shared a memory
I had not heard.

*When you were
a toddler
you looked up
to me and said:
Daddy, you are sweet
and you are good.*

Honey, he added
a name he'd never
used with me before
*I've been trying to live
up to that ever since.*

2.
Is it a daughter's duty
to remind fathers
to be sweet and good?

Are they dry creek beds
and we streams of water
that soften the soil?

Young and playful
do we gurgle through
their empty days?

Do we moisten
their spirits
and moods?

If so, how do we
measure and perceive
ourselves?

3.
Parenting guides praise
consistency. Dad was King
of Consistency:
        depreciation of others
        was his hobby
        his song and dance.
He refused
        art, music, sports
        anything of community,
so he could be
his natural self
a home body.

4.
Too often we felt
barefoot and calloused
my brothers
sister and I walking
on ragged rocks—
his be-littlings—
        tumbling —
our desires reduced
and tied to cost—
        how little we
        deserved—

      how generous
      he was in comparison.
He refused to celebrate
birthdays yet gave us money
each December.
He paid and repaid
our college educations
and when Mother
left cooking behind
he loved us through
meals he prepared
and raved about
      You won't find this
      at McDonald's,
he'd say.

Mom eventually drove away.
We were kept in place
slipping past him
as best we could.

5.
Children love to
collect pebbles,
      so comfortable
      in small hands
      treasures that shimmer
      precious as fears
      worn smooth
      by living against them.

Now I think of pebbles
as gifts for children
of fathers with dry spirits

dads who pass on
droughts from long ago
disappointments
day by day.

6.
Dad refuses
to invest
in a hearing aid.

He jokes,
always jokes:
> What do I need to hear
> at this age?
> I've heard it all before.

On his 92nd birthday
his memory loose
from shore,
he still asks:

*Just what are you doing
for work these days?*
I feel an ache
in my chest
unsettling
dizziness.
I confess
anyway, yelling
into the phone
as directed:
*I'm writing
a book of poetry.*

7.
Dad's reply tells me spirits inside
old bodies are not dry remains:

That's wonderful, he says.
Imagine,
we'll have
a published
author
in the family.

And there it is,
sweet and good,
his reply rock solid
to carry with me
in my palms.

The Day After Eighty-two Years Beyond The Great Depression

"Never met anyone as content with his own company
as your Dad," says his neighbor as she rises

from the chair unfolded for her in Papa's living room
leaving her paper plate with crumbs and a wadded napkin

in her place as she vacates before we begin
his memorial. After the front door closes behind her

we tell stories, remake Papa into an adventurer
who leaves upstate New York before we were born

to stake his claim on the West Coast just for us.
The day after, Papa's voice echoes as my sister

pulls the cord that opens the living room drapes
stirring spiders and webs. "We have a house to rent."

She hands me a dust rag. "Time is money. Make three
piles: things we keep; sell; give to the poor."

In the drawer beside his bathroom sink I scavenge
through plastic toothpicks, balls of tissues

Papa's boxes of matches and motel wrappers
melted to bars of soap, light as wafers in my palm.

Megaphone Song

Earth Mama's not meant for guns and drones
not meant to be the queen of war
or an open spigot of poverty and woe
for 60 million border crossers without homes

Earth's not a humvee, hum-bug or hum-drum
with 30 million homeless children on her back
she's not hiding out, not an extra terrestrial
telling war-orphaned kids to phone home

no matter how righteously we sell ourselves
guns in our trucks, mochas on our minds
arms to manufacture, troops to deploy
praying god's-on-our-side-thoughts at home

haunted refugees haunt Earth's bloody rivers
her land is not meant for killing grounds
haunted refugees haunting bloody rivers
Mama's soul, her soil, her growing fields

no matter how many ads or pills we swallow
how often we blink, or wink Hollywood eyes
or who the courts potty train, who gets off
Earth's not an injured spouse locked in a house

Earth's not stumping for political candidates
nor trading her banks off-shore for multi-takeovers
not investing in the greed of power-driven people
not preaching vanity to those destroying her home

Earth Mama's not a plaintiff city or nation
not a 607 billion dollar military theater
not an inspiring, risk-taking, star-lit beauty
more a megaphone weeping: *this is my home*

haunted refugees haunt Earth's bloody rivers
her land is not meant for killing grounds
haunted refugees haunting bloody rivers
Mama's soul, her soil, her growing fields

Earth's got no pocket book for bombs and drones
she's Mother Superior, heaving, weeping *not in my home*
Earth's got no pocket book for bombs and drones
Mother Superior heaves and weeps *this is my home*

haunted refugees haunt Earth's bloody rivers
her land is not meant for killing grounds
haunted refugees haunting bloody rivers
Mama's soul, her soil, her growing fields.

Simply Simplify

When you wake to the jolts and jives
broadcast from the race tracks of politics
the courts and rocking-horse news and
you're thinking *what's gonna happen next*

which horse should I bet on now and in
the turmoil your spirit breaks out in hives
then consider a more united state, a chorus
tuned to the Mickey Mouse Club song.

Simplify, simplify
Death's a-calling
Tomorrow's a-knocking
Today we simplify

The language of sounds
is a comet-like path
to memories
joyful and sad.

Amid uncertainties, we may be love-
struck, corny or angry-hot, yet our
feelings are still free and naturally
we're still bound to face adversities.

Simplify, simplify
Death's a-calling
Tomorrow's a-knocking
Today we simplify

When leaders promise to grab the reins
then reign from a bully pulpit, attempting
to turn millions into minions of citizen
bully puppets, tongues speaking hyperboles

put-downs, labels and psycho-babble-
analyses, then it is up to the chorus
to disavow and turn around for Earth runs
this race track, her foot-falls on our backs.

Disavow and turn around
For Death's a-calling
Tomorrow's a-knocking
Today we turn around

Like all species, people repeat and duplicate.
Human thoughts are mapped to mouths
that speak, hands that clap, feet that tap
and hearts that link to invisible chords

unmeasured. When humans protect
Earth's freedom of speech, to wed their
lives to the language of the Earth
her words become the offspring of the world.

Turn her Words into the World
Place your bets
Invest your spirit
Protecting Mother Earth

Now's the time to say hello

S-I-M-   M   ake good our work on Earth
P-L-Y-   Y   because Earth says so

Simply Simplify

    [Everybody's turn]

Simply Simplify

Paying Homage II

I kneel beside a flower bed
pull dandelions from the dirt

over my dog Mona Lisa's burial plot.
Above and behind us, a crow

crowns the Douglas fir
its caw an anxious code.

I find two gritty peanut shells
empty as flowerless vases

dust them off and when
I put them back, love

clings like dirt in the grooves
of my fingertips.

one day i was feeling oppressed and said right out loud

what's on your mind
tell me   just tell me
whatever's bothering you
get it off your chest

My chest replied …
"What took you so long to ask? Listen up …
You pay more attention to the demands
of your gut-factory with its boot-marching

"shoot-to-kill, loss of life, h-e-double-l
down on Earth commands for manufactured,
man-u're-fractured-words that produce
in me, your chest, regrets and spiritual death.

"Let fear go … listen in … to my factory.
I'm chief of efficiency and prosperous too.
Take a breath … right here … right now.
Notice your lungs and heart.

"See their innocence in pink.
We are your devoted partners.
You step to the beat of your lungs.
We pace each breath you take.

"It is time you notice our heroics.
Take heart … hear us … we are your ears,
when you listen, inside your art.
We are your beatific body central.

"Your Sistine Chapel of love.
Focus in ... take a breath ...
slow and deep ... tap into the sacred
in your chest, bow and vow

"to treasures you find ... right here ...
right now. Breathe, breathe deep and hold ...
breathe out ... feel your heart squeeze
and your lungs release Love unto the world."

Waking Spirit

Like an earthworm
God-forces pluck you
from the soil.

You so like a hungry bird
a Steller's jay, squawking
feed me, feed me.

Into Love's beak you go.
Don't be scared.
On this planet

there is a purpose
a reason for
highly sensitive beings.

Majestic Blue-black,
feel your wings spread
the wind beneath you

renewed anew
to fly and speak
fly and speak.

He Sails Us To Shore

     He sails toward me and waves
    risking bad grammar
   and sensual word-play.
One night, he types
  fantasies and promises
    half-naked, to wish
      and send sweet dreams.

     How easily, just one week
    he sails me, the steadfast one
   to erotic seas where
ocean waves crash
  on shore and stir up shells
    pebbles and sand at my feet
      before the waves retreat.

     He breezes in and breezes out—
    I am left empty, and still
   I believe in the rhythms
of ocean waves,
  their tumblings over rocks and sand
    where the white foam of sea matter
      retreats to muddier waters and returns.

    I won't find abandonment here
   nor love's abandon meant
  here, not where I imagine
God's soul, ever steadfast
  wearied-smooth as a pebble
    in gull wings and beaks, in winds
      that whisper and weep over shells and shore debris.

Demonstrations

1.

we take our healing slow
each act, every pill, dissolves
for better or worse into the past

we take our healing slow
every breath timely
a measured beat

a note in a symphony
a Joplin rag
an inner-city rap

New Orleans brass
big-city jazz
note after note repeating

where ever people gather
especially vigils
jails…death camps

we take our healing slow
as chicken broth
from feet and bones

simmering
each molecule
a collective sigh

2

In 1970, an era of student unrest
I was close to graduating from UCLA
newly-married, an English major with "A's"
if you exclude those English literature classes.

I still had Shakespeare to take.
Our professor, all 5'4" of him, wore jeans
his graying hair swept back in a pony tail
held by a leather band. Sitting on top

of a desk in front of the room, his feet
off the ground, swinging back and forth
he held our hands, brought Shakespeare
alive, waltzing through the life of the plays.

At the end of the quarter he prepared
us for the final: "You'll have two hours
to answer three essay questions.
Give me ideas I haven't yet considered."

"How can we do that?" we complained.

Slow and measured he replied:
"Cite Shakespeare's plays
and critics' insights with a depth
that also tells me about yourself."

Oh so Shakespearean of us—don't you think—
rebelling against the Vietnam war, armed
with megaphones and spirits, setting bon
fires, burning effigies, shutting the college down

during final's week, his dreaded exam canceled
saving my grade from certain descent.
Quarter ends with us swigging and swagging
between the internal and eternal question:

Is it nobler to be sparked by insights
inside a brick-walled classroom
or on the ground, deadlines swaying,
feet faithful to the arc of unrest?

An Earth Year Blessing

No man a salt shaker
No woman a sugar bowl

To pour, use up
Put out to pantry

No more darting of eyes
Or senator sneers

When Mama's Boys pilgrim
To Great Mama's pastures

To dance … step by step
With maternal wisdoms

Tango and waltz
Arms and heads in precision

Each foot-path a grace
Restoring Earth's faith

Mama's troupes swaying
Singing and praying …

Single Mama, Widowed Mama
Holy sustainer of lives

May we be a blessing to you
May your people tend, Dear Mama,

Dear Mama
Your people tend to you.

Canoe-Journey Moon

And yes, I search for the white sheets of peace
not worn or trumpeted, not full-bodied masks of hate

but billowing and clean on the universal laundry lines
the latitudes and longitudes of space and time

on this blue planet. And yes, the fractured nature
of unkind human traps of war: bomb blasts

drones, nuclear armaments (...*held off shore?*)
fracture me with anger, fear, and fretful sleep

until I drone into dis-belief. And yes, light takes flight
and never sleeps where neon filaments fill up

the black of night, that masquerade parade
in the market place of human trafficking.

And yes, in universal digital webs
the homeless-home of privacy charades.

And yet, tonight's full moon, lunar-majestic
still low on its canoe journey, drills a vortex

of shadows and lights into the depths of the Salish Sea.
On this still-ill night, I pull off the road

with a praise-full gasp
and offer ... *yes* ... and ... *yes*...

Bless Thee

Bless the permanence and impermanence of sleep
Bless the permanence and impermanence of wind gusts
Bless the permanence and impermanence of blinding rain
Bless the permanence and impermanence of floods

Bless the Buddha, bless His Holiness the Dalai Lama
Bless the monsoons at Rato Monastery, Mundgod, India
Bless the rootedness of rootless refugees
Bless chains-of-good-bye-good-night-moons

Bless the monks' footfalls over Himalayas through Nepal
Bless India for providing them homes
Bless saffron tea, crimson-rose-and-ocher-dyed robes
Bless humming monks, lifting us up…like tea cups

Bless guru root teacher Khyongla Rato Rinpoche
Bless the Tibet Center of New York
Bless his first students, bless their legacies: Joseph Campbell
Richard Gere, Beastie Boy Adam, and Nicky Vreeland

Bless Nicky's rain-splattered reign as Abbot of Rato Monastery
Bless humble-eye-attachments to cameras and lenses
Bless two-thousand-five-hundred-year-old longings for enlightenment
Bless the twilight, peaceful phrase: *I prefer to see joy this way*

Bless potential Buddha natures blessing the desuetude
Bless tumbling tides, legs of the Moon, arms of the Sun
Bless every lost and found water-bottle dawn
Bless teacup-hearts coming home, humming love
Bless thee.

Metamorphosis

I think of earthworms
plucked from grief's soil

steller's jays squawking
feed me   feed me

magpies inspiring rhymes
in the sorrowbird's song

parrots perching
beside comedians' hearts

bower birds building nest eggs
with scraps of art

while cardinals spread holy wings
riding oceanic waves

old world cranes migrate
with deep-throated blues

peacocks strut … belt out mating calls
neon eyespots flashing

hawks with military precision
test infinity … hungry

as financiers of the new world's beak
swallow entire species

yet before spiders in the dark of debris
inherit earth's rubble

birds rise up in flocks, wing their way
to nature's spawning grounds all a-twitter

to bow and warble ... bow and warble
nest and feed ... nest and feed.

I Woke One Morning

For those who lose loved ones to suicide

1.
Before she died in 2009, Silversong Belcourt spoke:

*I was taught the way to honor
is through living your passion,
the door to your passion
is through a deep pain,
and the door to understanding
is through your deepest wound.*

*If you want to know your life's purpose,
find your deepest pain,
and in it will be
what is missing for you.*

II.
I woke one morning
and heard an ancestral voice:

*Life itself is very important.
We must deliver ourselves to the confusion.*

For a decade I delivered myself
to bags of worry

with plans to out-smart
our culture's rising tides of suicides.

To prevent more loss of lives,
I reported statistics of those who died.

To schools and clinics I brought
prevention programs.

To the public I taught warning signs.
On the phone, I consoled those left to survive.

Now with each new suicide
I resolve as life does to travel

slow-step-by-slow-step
through despair and grief

to those thin places, where
sometimes through silence,

sometimes through chaos,
ancestral voices speak to us.

I travel there with you, dear neighbor,
whenever we talk heart.

III.
As I wake thin places are warm showers, bubbly
dishwater, and meal making in my kitchen sanctuary
with its roots to great grandmothers.

I relish long drives, quiet walks, full-moon
mornings and first wakings when I say:
"Today something wonderful will come my way."

I once longed for the money
found today in asphalt parking lots
of corporate playgrounds.

Instead I deliver myself to the open mics
of cedars and pines where the Ancient Ones
gather their quiet-mind-stories.

You'll find them smiling most readably
in crystals of light on moss,
raindrops on arms of ferns unfolding.

Beneath February's Slivered Moon

I wake at dawn to sun and ice
roadway diamonds.

In my yard two deer, displaced-thin
nibble on clover.

I too am rail thin, a short path away
from a milestone birthday, and in

this quiet moment, this devoted stretch
of first-waking thoughts

electricity and love spark.
I listen kindly to circuits.

Central Healing

After many Moons, people divested of all but their dignity arrive
knees and backs bend to stick hands into oily waters:

> *On sacred tribal lands*
> *Bear Dancers circle round*
> *Bend, grunting toward the ground*

world leaders sweat beneath the Sun to save sea life and gulls
oil execs and railroad owners strain their muscles to vacuum up debris

wall streeters trade themselves to protect the riches of the sea
even journalists stop their broadcasts to plant, harvest and seed

> *White sage smolders*
> *Drums beat and Elders speak*
> *Of wintering the past*

for beyond Katrina, beyond tsunamis
beyond depletion of herring, sea scooters, salmon and orcas

beyond deregulations, housing foreclosures, lost savings
beyond meager health care, minor energy reforms

> *Give your pain to the Bears*
> *Give it up to the fire*
> *Flames crackle, spark and rise*

beyond contamination of world-wide food supplies
beyond viral buyouts of commerce, media, banks

beyond nuclear meltdowns, trains de-railing
carbon counts rising, glaciers melting, oceans warming

> *Give your pain to the bears*
> *Give it up to the fire*
> *Drums beat and Elders speak*

beyond the blow out of safety valves on the pipes of democracy
beyond the sludge of remorse, the rattle of bones

Mother Time draws the line at Cherry Point and Salish Sea
home of tribal wisdoms and sovereign treaties

> *Give your pain to the Bears*
> *Give it up to the fire*
> *We mourn, shuffle, weave and dance*

and in this far west corner, we the people of many nations
beholden, as we are, to the great Salish Sea

recall the taste of wild salmon, waters safe for drinking
clean air, and old growth trees

> *Give your pain to the Bears*
> *Give it up to the fire*
> *We trail, track, circle round*

and, as Sun and Moon rise over Time's rail line,
hearts pulse and echo nature's drum beats …

We trail, track, circle round
Bend grunting toward the ground
Flames of love spark and rise

and with a Motherly rush, we return like salmon, swim upstream restoring Mother Earth's forests, rivers and seas

Love abounds in Elder nations
Love abounds in citizen nations
On planet earth, love abounds.

A Northwest Winter's Dream

I do not know how I arrived
on this mountain or where we are destined
but my car is filled with passengers.
On a red-soiled road, we climb
wheels spinning crushing rock. When we
reach the summit, the cliff edge beckons.
My car could sprout wings but I swerve
from ledge and air and wake up scared.

How mute, this day-break, how silent
this call to change my way on my distant
brother's birthday. While trees pine
in greens and browns, the sky in empty gray
moon light shimmers through my bedroom's shade
and I breathe in the awe of dawn.

The Poet's Legacy

> *With the phrase — 'keep up your courage, old son'—*
> *I was given hope, empowered by a sense of solidarity*
> *not only with the spirit of my father but with other voices*
> *that have gone before, among them the voices of poetry.*
> —Michael Dennis Browne

On the day before Halloween
the Pacific Northwest wore
a mourner's black-hooded coat

dark comfort
from pelting rains,
autumn's leave-takings.

In silent remembrance
a woman crosses a parking lot,
whispers, prayerfully:

Happy Birthday, Mom.
You are loved,
mourned, missed.

What are you doing here?
a motherly voice intrudes
as though admonishing her.

A decade later, beneath
the cloak and hood of clouds,
What are you doing here?!

she weeps, breathes, still believes
in the Vigil of Poets
their chorus, singing:

Whenever your heart mourns,
Keep us near,
Keep us near.

Notes to the Poems

"A Note To Readers": *the bell tolls* comes from "For Whom the Bell Tolls" by John Donne.

"Central Heating": If only there were a mathematical formula that could resolve the debate over humankind's impact on earth.

"Great To Be": The word a-w-e-d, sounds a lot like o-d-d. That can't be helped, as you will see.

"Great To Be II": I play with words, the poet's tools, and believe there can be more than one structure to enhance a poem. Here "Great to Be" becomes a dedication "for the nonce," in appreciation of the musical artistry of pianist Cindy Minkler.

"A Courtroom And A Waterfall": Dedicated to Calene LeBeau, who in a few short years had a significant effect in our community when she served as director of the Community Foundation. With appreciation to Rob Stoops, a scholar and first reader of several poems.

"Betty Goes To Yoga": Like the actress Betty White, when my mother was in her 80s, she said: "When I look in the mirror, I cannot believe the face staring back belongs to me."

"Dear Fred": For Fred Fragner (1915-2009) with homage to *Daddy Long Legs* author Jean Webster (1876-1916) whom I hope and imagine after meeting Fred (if that were possible) would reconsider her favorable stance regarding eugenics for "solving" social problems. Adelaide Crapsey (1878-1914) and Webster were roommates at Vassar and reportedly, Adelaide was the inspiration behind the heroine in *Daddy Long Legs*. Adelaide created the American cinquain: a five-line form modeled after the Japanese tanka, comprised of 5 lines totaling 22 syllables, shaped: 2, 4, 6, 8, 2.

"After Words I" and "After Words II": Also dedicated to Czechoslovakian-born Fred Fragner (1915-2009) who survived Buchenwald and with his first wife Kay brought 60 orphaned children to the U.S. in 1946.

"Savings", "My Dog Barks", "Paying Homage I and II": In honor of our
    family dachshund; her ever-feisty, ever-present loving voice lives on.
"Beyond Capricorn and Cancer": Won first place in the Kumquat Challenge,
    Spring 2014. Incorporates the words, "reflect;hold;zone;yield;
    fall;tear;quick;shade;key;carry."
"After His Sister Dies": For Rob.
"Roots And Seeds": Incorporates words from the 2013 edition of the
    Kumquat Challenge which include: "burn; chime; cotton; drift;
    flight; kind; moment; offer; signal and volume." Poem is shaped to
    portray thinking that puts observations into categories as juxtaposed
    to the symbiotic interweave found in the natural world and often in
    spiritual beliefs.
"May Peace Become Us": The words: *Honoring and acknowledging
    Lhaq'temish Traditional Territories / since time immemorial
    Lhaq'temish, "the People"/ have lived in these territories* are those of
    the Lummi Nation.
"My Middle Finger": Written from a prompt given by Kelli Russell Agodon
    on behalf of the Sue Boynton Poetry Contest. The prompt: *Write
    about an imperfect body part.*
"Dear Cake and Bake": Written from a prompt given by Kelli Russell
Agodon to inspire creative leaps and unique connections. Five
    instructions and five words given to me by fellow participant Karen
    Vande Bossche.
"Husbandry": The italicized headings from a reading by Priscilla Long,
    Whatcom County Museum, Feb. 28, 2014, in conjunction with the
    Vanishing Ice art exhibit.
"On The Day I Prayed to Mother Mary": After writing the poem, I learned
    the lady bug is a mythological symbol for the Mother Mary.
"The Foghorn": Written on Earth Day, April 22, 2015; performed with
    appreciation to Matthew Brouwer, Kevin Murphy and JP Falcon
    Grady.
"A Poet Prays For Peace": Rumi (1207-1273) Translated by Coleman Barks,
    written in syllabics.
"Portals": A Galilee porch is an image that I did not understand when the
    words came to me; I still do not know how to unravel the reference,

so many themes are embedded in the history of the words. A Galilee porch is a vestibule on the west side of medieval cathedrals where penitents were greeted and allowed to enter the sanctuary; often women greeted by priests, entering the west wing. A Galilee porch refers also to the promenade on decks of ocean liners. Some readers may also think of the Sea of Galilee where much of the ministry of Jesus occurred. According to Wikipedia, sadly, this fresh water lake which divides Israel and Jordan has sustained years of drought. Low water levels have stressed the lake's ecology and species are facing extinction. I also suspect the poem might have something to do with the will to live and the portal one might cross when facing one's own death.

"Ducks Fly": Dedicated to Carol Howe, who along with her husband Jim were two of the original founders of the National Alliance on Mental Illness. Jim served as national president. With gratitude for their friendship and leadership after retirement here in Whatcom County.

"In God He Trusts; In Sleep He Trysts with Death," and "Dry Creek Beds And Streams": Dedicated to my dad.

"Simply Simplify": A performance poem. JP Falcon Grady sings the italicized lyrics.

"one day i was feeling oppressed and said right out loud": A performance poem with JP.

"Demonstrations": After seeing "Every War Has Two Losers" a tribute to William Stafford in a workshop led by Carla Shafer.

"Canoe Journey Moon": Written from a prompt given by Rebecca Mabanglo-Mayor at Whatcom Peace and Justice Center. Dedicated to Richard Jehn (1950-2016).

"Bless Thee": written from a prompt given by Priscilla Long. Inspired after viewing *Monk with a Camera: The Life and Journey of Nicholas Vreeland.*

"I Woke One Morning": Before Silversong Belcourt (1944-2009) died of cancer, she founded the Indigenous Studies Foundation. The visionary behind Honor Day celebrated on August 20th, she built peace through respect for all peoples,

"A Northwest Winter's Dream": A tribute to William Stafford. For my brother who shares the same birth date and month, named after our uncle, a navy seaman who died by suicide, a drowning, after serving in World War II.

About The Author

Betty Scott's poems are influenced by California, Oregon and Washington landscapes. She earned degrees from U.C.L.A., Central Washington University and Western Washington University and taught in community colleges before retiring into her daily writing life. She enjoys editing her daughter's novels as well as poetry and essays by colleagues in Bellingham, WA. She is currently writing a third collection of poems and a book of essays.

www.ingramcontent.com/pod-product-compliance
Lightning Source LLC
Chambersburg PA
CBHW051654040426
42446CB00009B/1139